Legacy of Love

A Kids' Christmas Musical about Lasting Love

by **Katie Combs**
Arranged by **Dave Clark**

Performance time: 39 minutes

lillenaskids

lillenaskids.com

Cast

Webcast Hosts

Jim: Adult or older child with a polished, energetic speaking voice

Krista: Adult or older child with a polished, energetic speaking voice

Mega Media Club Members

Grace: Older girl; Organized and efficient

Julian: Technical guru

Matt: Sensitive big brother type

Casey: Fun and friendly

Samantha: Sweet and caring

Joey: Witty and fun

Kerri: Bubbly and perky

Mr. Thompson: Loving, energetic teacher who is passionate about Christmas and his love for his students

Set stage requirements: Mega Media Clubhouse, Town Square, Webcast Booth (optional)

Contents

Christmas Groove

Words and Music by
KATIE COMBS
Arr. by Dave Clark

(Lights up. Choir enters as music begins.)

Driving ♩ = ca. 124

CD: 1

CHOIR *unis.*

Got-ta

13

jump, jump,— jump; got-ta move, move,— move. O you

F

E♭2

15

can't stand— still when the Spir - it— moves— you. Got-ta

Gm7

F/A

B♭

B♭/C

17

give love— out, you got noth-ing to— lose; 'Cause

F

E♭2

CD: 3 *2nd time*

2nd time: GROUP 2

19

Christ - mas puts— you in the giv - in' groove.— Got-ta

Gm7

F/A

B♭/C

F

21

Slide in - to gen - er - os - i - ty,

2nd time: GROUP 2

jump, jump, jump; Got-ta move, move, move;

C | F/A

23

swing your heart o - pen;

Swing, swing, swing; When the Spir - it moves you. Got-ta

Dm7 | Gm7

CD: 2 1st time

CD: 4 2nd time

25

Spin a - round and you will see that

give love out, you got noth-ing to lose. 'Cause

Eb2

27

(to pg. 6, meas. 13)

giv - ing leaves___ a leg - a - cy.___ Got - ta

Christ - mas puts___ you in the giv - in' groove.___ Got - ta

(to pg. 6, meas. 13)

$\frac{C}{E}$ C

29

jump, jump,___ jump; got - ta move, move,___ move. O you

F E♭2

31

can't stand___ still when the Spir - it___ moves___ you. Got - ta

G m7 $\frac{F}{A}$ B♭ $\frac{B♭}{C}$

CD: 5

33

give love__ out, you got noth-ing to__ lose; 'Cause

F   E♭2

35

Christ - mas puts__ you in the giv - in' groove. So

Gm7   F/A   B♭/C   F

37

jump, slide,

Gm7   F/A

39

spin, glide.

B♭   F/A

CD: 6

41

Come with me___ en - joy___ the ride.___

$E\flat 2$

43

Sing a - long___ just one___ more time.___ Got - ta

$\frac{C}{E}$

C

45

jump, jump,__ jump; got - ta move, move,__ move. O you

N.C.

F

$E\flat 2$

47

can't stand__ still when the Spir - it__ moves___ you. Got - ta

$G m^7$

$\frac{F}{A}$

$B\flat$

$\frac{B\flat}{C}$

CD: 7
49
give love out, you got noth-ing to lose; 'Cause
N.C.
F
E♭2
51
Christ - mas puts you in the giv - in' groove. Got-ta
Gm7
F/A
B♭/C
F
53
jump, jump, jump; got-ta move, move, move. O you
E♭2
55
can't stand still when the Spir - it moves you. Got-ta
Gm7
F/A
B♭
B♭/C

57

give love out, you got noth-ing to lose; 'Cause

F

E♭2

59 CD: 8

Christ - mas puts you in the giv - in' groove. 'Cause

G m7

F/A

B♭/C

F

61

Christ - mas puts you in the giv - in' groove. 'Cause

G m7

F/A

B♭/C

D m7

63

Christ - mas puts you in the

G m7

F/A

B♭

giv - in' groove.

Scene 1

(Lights up on Mega Media Clubhouse. KIDS are working at the computers and hanging out.)

JULIAN: So, did you catch yesterday's Kids for Christ webcast?

GRACE: No, I missed it. Anything new?

JULIAN: Yeah, they said they had some new announcement to make today.

GRACE: Cool! I wonder what it could be?

JULIAN: I don't know.

MATT: Has anyone seen Mr. Thompson?

KERRI: He should be here any second. He's probably out decorating the rest of the school. You know how crazy he is about Christmas!

(ALL agree. MR. THOMPSON enters wearing outlandish Christmas clothes and a silly Christmas hat.)

MR. THOMPSON: Ho ho ho! Merry Christmas!!

(KIDS ad lib greetings.)

MR. THOMPSON: How's my Mega Media Club today? Enjoying the season? I love Christmas, did you know that?

(KIDS laugh.)

MR. THOMPSON: So Casey, what's on the agenda for today?

CASEY: Well Mr. Thompson, today we were going to upload some school pictures for the website.

MR. THOMPSON: Nice, nice. I'm trying to organize some caroling for later this week; I hope I can count you kids in. You know, Mrs. Thompson always used to organize the caroling before she got sick. I know that she'd want us to continue all those wonderful traditions. She's one of the few people that actually loved Christmas more than I did. I know the best way to honor her memory is to continue to do the work she loved! So can I count you all in?

(ALL agree.)

MR. THOMPSON: Great! I have to run back to the office and check on some things. You kids get started on those photos and I'll double-check your work when I get back.

JOEY: Sure thing Mr. Thompson!

(MR. THOMPSON exits.)

SAM: I'll get started on those photos!

GRACE: Hey, isn't it almost time for the Kids for Christ webcast?

JULIAN: Yeah, I'll pull it up right now!

("Kids for Christ Theme Song" begins. Lights up on Webcast Booth. Announcers can be visible on a separate part of the stage framed out to look like a monitor screen or have voice over style parts off stage. Mega Media members crowd around the monitor to watch the webcast.)

Kids for Christ Theme Song

Music by
TIM HIGINBOTHAM
Arr. by Dave Clark

JIM: Good afternoon kids, I trust your Christmas season has been filled with joy and merriment so far! I'm Jim . . .

KRISTA: . . . And I'm Krista! And we want to welcome you back to Kids for Christ! Hope your weekend was fabulous!

JIM: Now as we mentioned yesterday, we've got a big announcement to make today. So we want to stir the Christmas pot, so to speak, and get you thinking on this one . . .

KRISTA: Christmas is a time of receiving, but it's also a time of great giving. Think for a moment about what each of you is thankful for this Christmas . . .

JIM: Now think of the great God who makes all that possible!

KRISTA: Kinda mind blowing, isn't it?

JIM: Yes it is, Krista! And to think for Christmas He gave you the most amazing Christmas present ever . . . His son!

KRISTA: So the Kids for Christ producers here were thinking . . . what's a way we could encourage you kids to really be Kids for Christ?

JIM: And the answer was simple . . .

(Music begins. Lights up on choir.)

Leave a Mark

Words and Music by
KATIE COMBS
Arr. by Dave Clark

1. We've been giv - en op - por - tun - i - ty___ To
2. There's a teach - er who taught us to give;___

11

make a dif - f'rence so come on with me.___
Gave His life___ so that we all could live.___ The

D♭   Fm

CD: 11 *1st time*
CD: 13 *2nd time*

13

Take the time___ to give un - sel - fish - ly And we
great - est leg - a - cy for you, for me; He gave

Fm   B♭m

15

cresc.   *f*

can leave a leg - a - cy.   O
His life to set___ us free.

A♭   C

cresc.   *f*

17

I wan-na leave a mark___ and be a light shin-ing thro' the dark___

Fm   B♭m   D♭2

___ So get on board and bring your heart,___ we'll leave our mark.

E♭sus   E♭   Fm   B♭m

20

Ev - 'ry boy and girl___ can leave an

Fm   C   Fm   B♭m

CD: 12 *1st time*
CD: 14 *2nd time*

22

im - print on the world___ And now's the per - fect time to start___

D♭2   E♭sus   E♭   Fm

to leave a mark.

So take your time___ and give it out; Take your love,

___ pass it a-round. You will find___ with-out a doubt

That leg - a - cy___ is what love's___ a - bout. O

34

I wan-na, I wan-na, I wan-na, I wan-na, I wan-na leave a mark.

Fm   B♭m   Fm

I wan-na, I wan-na, I wan-na, I wan-na,

B♭m   Fm   B♭m

37

I wan-na leave a mark.   I wan-na leave a mark

Fm   B♭m   Fm

____ and be a light shin-ing thro' the dark___ So get on

B♭m   D♭2   E♭sus   E♭

40

board and bring your heart,__ we'll leave our mark.

Fm   B♭m   Fm   C

42

Ev - 'ry boy and girl__ can leave an im - print on the world__

Fm   B♭m   D♭2

CD: 16

__ And now's the per - fect time to start__ to leave a mark.

E♭sus   E♭   Fm   B♭m

45

I wan - na, I wan - na,

Fm   C   Fm

I wan-na, I wan-na, I wan-na leave a mark.

B♭m   Fm   B♭m

48

I wan-na, I wan-na, I wan-na, I wan-na, I wan-na leave a mark.

Fm   B♭m   Fm

I wan-na, I wan-na, I wan-na, I wan-na,

B♭m   Fm   B♭m

51

I wan-na leave a mark.   I wan-na, I wan-na,

Fm   B♭m   Fm

I wan-na, I wan-na, I wan-na leave a mark.

JIM: So kids- what's it gonna be?

KRISTA: Are you ready to give back to the One who gave it all?

JIM: And the big announcement is . . . drum roll please . . .

KRISTA: This year we are sponsoring a "Leave a Mark" contest!

JIM: Yes, you heard right, a "Leave a Mark" contest!

KRISTA: So here are the rules: You have one week to come up with a variety of ways to show Christ's love in service to others. This is how the "Leave a Mark" contest works . . . it's all about passing on Christ's love on to others.

JIM: Think for a minute about all those people in your life that have shown you God's love. They have given you gifts; of time, or things that are special to you . . . and now is your chance to pay it forward. So send us your ideas and document your service. The team that does the best job wins the grand prize . . . a brand new laptop computer!

KRISTA: So kids, get out there! Get creative! Show God's love in as many ways you can think of! It's your turn to leave your own "mark" this Christmas.

JIM: Good luck and God bless!

(Lights out on webcast announcers.)

KERRI: Wow! That sounds fun!

(MR. THOMPSON enters.)

MR. THOMPSON: Hey kids, how are the photos going?

CASEY: Going great, Mr. T. Almost uploaded . . . wanna check?

MR. THOMPSON: Sure, let me just plug in my laptop and take a look . . . oh no!!

MATT: What is it, Mr. T.?

MR. THOMPSON: It looks like my hard drive is fried! Well it doesn't surprise me. Mrs. Thompson was on me for years to replace this one. But what bad timing- right at Christmas . . . phooey! Let me go see if I can borrow Mrs. Heisner's laptop- I'll be right back.

(MR. THOMPSON exits.)

SAM: So are you thinking what I'm thinking?

JOEY: That we're out of chips?

SAM: No! About Mr. Thompson!

JOEY: He has chips?

SAM: No, goofy! He needs a laptop!

JOEY: Still not following . . . he needs a laptop to eat chips? Oh wait, to order chips online!

KERRI: No, Mr. Thompson needs a new laptop!

JOEY *(teasing)*: And the webcast contest can win us one!

CASEY: That would be a great Christmas present!

GRACE: This has to be hard on Mr. Thompson anyway . . . his first Christmas without Mrs. Thompson.

KERRI: And he loves Christmas so much!

JOEY: So what are we waiting for?

MATT: Let's win us a laptop!

SAM: It won't be easy.

GRACE: We've got to be super creative!

CASEY: We'd better get started!

GRACE: Don't worry, my mom says I'm the queen of initiative!

MATT: What's that?

JOEY: Is that the country where they invented chips?

(ALL *laugh*.)

GRACE: No, silly, it means seeing what needs to be done and doing it!

JOEY: Oh, I'm all over that!

JULIAN: Yeah, let's make it happen!

(*Fade to black*.)

Scene 2

(*Media members exit quickly and stand outside the door with props. "Kids for Christ Theme Song" may be played at this time. Lights up on the Mega Media Clubhouse. KIDS enter media room exhausted; holding brooms, mops, trash bags, and assorted cleaning equipment.*)

MATT: Whew! I'm exhausted!

KERRI: You're not kidding!

GRACE: I had no idea this work would be so much . . . well . . . work!

SAM: Isn't that kind of the point?

JOEY: I need some candy!

CASEY: Whose idea was it to clean the community center anyway?

(ALL *turn to* MATT.)

MATT: Hey! Don't get all over me . . . you thought it was a great idea when we wrote it down!

JULIAN: Yeah, but who knew the place would be trashed from the Community Yard Sale!

JOEY: At least we got it done. We can check it off our list.

GRACE: Remember what we're doing this for.

SAM: Yeah . . . Mr. Thompson. This will mean so much to him.

CASEY: OK, so where are we on our list?

JULIAN (*holding video camera*): I'll upload today's project to the webcast. Sam, you ready to report?

SAM: Yep!

JULIAN: OK, you're on.

SAM (*on camera*): Hey all. Today we "made our mark" by pitching in to clean the community center. We figured we had so many people taking care of us . . . picking up after us all the time that we'd pass it on. More to come tomorrow. Over and out.

JULIAN: Great job, Sam!

MATT: Let's pick something easy this time!

KERRI: Wait a minute. This is about showing Christ's love . . . He didn't pick the easy way.

CASEY: Yeah, that's true. I guarantee whatever you can think of . . . He's done bigger things!

JOEY: Hey, I like that. "God's done bigger things"! It has a ring to it . . .

(*Music begins. Lights up on choir. During song choir puts on sunglasses. See the "Legacy of Love Director's Resource" for additional movement ideas.*)

God's Done Bigger Things

KATIE COMBS

NICK ROBERTSON
and KATIE COMBS
Arr. by Dave Clark

CD: 17

Rap feel ♩ = ca. 112

Dm

mf

Dm

Dm

CHOIR *unis.*
mf

1. Let me share___ with you some his - to - ry; The
2. All the maj - es - ty of Christ - mas lights

Dm Gm Dm Gm

Bi - ble's packed___ with lots of mys - er - y. So
Can't com - pare___ to all the stars at night.

Dm   Gm   Dm   Gm

CD: **18** *1st time*

CD: **20** *2nd time*

get in - spired___ by the King of kings; It's true,
Na - ture's filled___ with some a - maz - ing sights.

Dm   Gm   Dm   Gm

there's proof. God's___ done big-ger things.

Dm   N.C.

God's_____ done big-ger things.

O_____ He's done big-ger things.

CD: 21 *2nd time*

God's_____ done big-ger things.

CD: 19 *1st time*

1

(to pg. 28, meas. 9)

25
2
He walked on wa - ter and He
Dm
Gm7
27
raised the dead; The sick were healed and the
Am7
Dm7
Gm7
29
hun - gry fed. The wind and waves o - beyed each
Am7
Dm7
Gm7
31
CD: 22
word He said; So no mat - ter what you do,
Am7
Dm7
B♭

GROUP 1

God's___ done big-ger things.

GROUP 2

He's still work - ing, He's not

A

D m

God's___ done big-ger things.

done;

Great - er things___ are still to

D m

come.

O___ He's done big-ger things.

Get ex - cit - ed 'bout the

D m

JULIAN: Does everyone have their assignments for tomorrow?

(ALL agree.)

JULIAN: OK, let's meet back here . . .

(MR. THOMPSON enters.)

MR. THOMPSON: You on your way out?

(All kids exit leaving MATT and MR. THOMPSON. MR. THOMPSON notices that MATT is still there and approaches him.)

MR. THOMPSON: All right, see you guys. *(Beat)* You OK? I couldn't help but notice you seem kinda down today.

MATT: Well, Mr. T., I'm kinda dreading going home.

MR. THOMPSON: Why is that Matt?

MATT: You remember how my grandma passed away last Spring?

MR. THOMPSON: Yeah.

MATT: Well, every Christmas my grandmother would have us all over and we would eat cookies while she and grandpa would read the Christmas story. Sometimes we'd even act it out. It may sound kinda silly, but we all looked forward to it.

MR. THOMPSON: That sounds awfully nice . . .

MATT: Well, it was, but now my mom is insisting that grandpa come to our house and we bake cookies and read the story and I just think that it is going to be, well . . .

MR. THOMPSON: Too sad with your grandmother gone?

MATT: Yeah . . . exactly

MR. THOMPSON: You know, I know exactly how you feel. This is my first year without Mrs. Thompson. Boy, did she love Christmas. *(Music begins.)* Holidays can be especially hard when you can't be with the ones you love. But, have you ever heard of the legacy of love?

MATT: The what?

MR. THOMPSON: The legacy of love . . . let me explain.

(Lights up on choir.)

Legacy of Love

KATIE COMBS

NICK ROBERTSON
and KATIE COMBS
Arr. by Dave Clark

CD: 23

Half-time feel ♩ = ca. 66

1. There are peo - ple in_____ our lives_____
(2. There's a) Fa - ther who_____ loves chil -

1st time: MR. THOMPSON *freely*
2nd time: CHOIR

10
for just a sea - son;
- dren with - out ques - tion;
D/F♯
A sus
12
They watch us grow and love
And He knows each hair on ev -
A
G
14
us as we are.
- 'ry child's head.
B m
A sus

16

And when they step a - way___ you see___
And when He steps a - way___ He sees___

A   G²

18

___ a bril - liant tap - es - try;
___ a bril - liant tap - es - try.

D/F♯   Em⁷

20

An im - print on___ our lives___
A world in need___ of love's___

D/F♯   C

CD: **24** *1st time*

CD: **26** *2nd time*

1st time: SOLO *and* CHOIR
2nd time: CHOIR *mf*

22

that shows___ their heart. It's the
re - deem - ing gift.

G/B   A sus   A

25

leg - a - cy___ of love___ and it's___ a - maz - ing;

D sus   D   D/F♯   G

mf

28

And ev - er chang - ing as___ the sand___ a - long___ the shore.

G   D/F♯   E m⁷   G²

31
And if you
A sus
A
33
hold those mem - o - ries in - side your
(2) prom - is - es
D sus
D
35
heart you take a hold of the gift, their
G
A
B m
E m7
38
CD: 27 2nd time
1
leg - a - cy of love.
G 2
A
D
A
B
B m

41

A/G G A sus

45

(to pg. 35, meas. 9) 2

CHOIR *unis.* *mp*

2. There's a

A sus A D

cresc.

48

f

It's the   leg - a - cy___ of love___ and it's___ a - maz-

Ab/Bb Bb Eb sus Eb Eb/G

f

51

- ing;   And ev - er chang - ing as___ the sand

Ab Eb/G F m7

54
a - long the shore.
And if you
Fm7 A♭2 B♭sus B♭
57
hold those prom - is - es in - side your
E♭sus E♭
59
heart you take a hold of the gift, their
A♭ B♭ Cm Fm7
62
leg - a - cy of love.
A♭2 B♭ E♭ E♭sus

Scene 3

(Lights up Mega Media Clubhouse. Cast enters with stuff: clothing, toys, bags, etc.)

SAM: Wow! That's a lot of stuff!

GRACE: We better get organized.

KERRI: Yeah, this is great. I never thought we would get so much for the clothing and toy donation box in just a day.

JOEY: Who's in charge here?

SAM: Why don't you help us out?

JOEY: OK . . . but it'll cost you some M&Ms!!!

CASEY: Let's make a couple of piles: toys, clothes, kitchen stuff . . . what else?

(Music begins. Light up on choir. During song Media Club members organizes and sorts all the stuff into the labeled donation boxes.)

Little Bit of Stuff

KATIE COMBS

NICK ROBERTSON
and KATIE COMBS
Arr. by Dave Clark

CD: 28

Funky ♩ = ca. 105

CHOIR *unis.*

Get a lit-tle bit of

9

stuff,   stuff,   stuff;   When you see that it's e - nough, nough,   nough.

Then you find some - one in   need,   need,   need;   And you give it joy - ful -

12

ly,   ly,   ly.   And you're spread - ing out the   love, love,— love;

It's re - flect - ing what's a - bove,   bove,— bove.   And it

CD: 33 *3rd time*

3rd time to Coda ⊕
(to pg. 47, meas. 29)

all be - gan with a lit-tle bit of stuff.

C

F

CD: 29 *1st time*

CD: 31 *2nd time*

2. So

B♭

C

F

1. Christ - mas___ re - minds us___ of a
give out___ a love for___ a

B♭

F/A

23

Bb ... F ... F/A

all the stuff___ we think___ we need.___ But That
Sav - ior born___ for you___ and me.___ That

CD: 30 *1st time*
CD: 32 *2nd time*

25

Bb ... F/A

God's plan___ is big - ger,___ it's
gives us___ new life for

Repeat twice
(to pg. 44, meas. 9)

27

C/E ... C

grand - er that___ we see.___ Get a lit - tle bit of
all e - ter - ni - ty.___

29 CODA

stuff.　　　　Give　a　help - ing＿ hand,＿＿

F　　　　　　Dm　　　C　　　B♭

32

fol - low God's com - mand;＿＿

Dm　　　　　　C　　　B♭

34

You　will find＿＿　　peace　of mind＿＿　　as　you

C/E　　　　　　　　Am　　　B♭

36　CD: 34

lay　　up　treas - ure.　　　Get a lit - tle bit of

B♭　　C/B♭　　B♭/D　　C

39

stuff, stuff, stuff; When you see that it's e-nough, nough, nough.

Then you find some-one in need, need, need; And you give it joy-ful-

42

ly, ly, ly. And you're spread-ing out the love, love,— love;

It's re-flect-ing what's a-bove, bove,— bove. And it

all be - gan with a lit-tle bit of stuff.

(KIDS exit with stuff. Fade to black.)

Scene 4

("Kids for Christ Theme Song" may be used to allow for scene transition. Lights up. KIDS are hanging out in Mega Media Clubhouse.)

GRACE *(sitting at the computer)*: So, I'm looking at the podcast rating and we are in the top three!!!

SAM: Should we let Mr. T. in on what were doing?

JULIAN: Well, I think he has his suspicions.

JOEY: He asked me what I was doing with all these clothes and I said I was cleaning out my attic. He just winked and said, "Yeah, sure . . . I don't remember you wearing this" . . . and pulled out your sister's pink feathered hat! He's on to us!

KERRI: Oh . . . how I want to give him that computer!

(MR. THOMPSON enters in an even more outlandish Christmas outfit.)

MR. THOMPSON: Merry Christmas!!! How my Mega Media Club today?

(MR. THOMPSON starts to wander around the media room.)

MATT: We're great, Mr. T, and we are working on those graphics you asked for!

(MR. THOMPSON *picks up a brownie mix box.*)

MR. THOMPSON: Sure looks like you kids are hungry! What's all this?

JOEY: You know Mr. T, we are growing, growing! You don't get these kinda muscles from not eating! (JOEY *flexes his arm.*)

MR. THOMPSON: Well, I don't know anyone that got muscles from . . . uh . . . brownie mix.
(KIDS *look around at each other nervously*) That's cool. You kids don't want to tell me what your up to? *(Winking)* I'm pretty sneaky myself . . . and uh, don't forget to save me a brownie! Keep up the great work!

(MR. THOMPSON *exits.*)

GRACE: That was close!

SAM: We better get started. Those brownies aren't going to make themselves.

CASEY: I hope the kids at the Children's Center like chocolate.

KERRI: Who doesn't like chocolate??

JULIAN: If Joey doesn't eat all the mix!

JOEY: Hey? Are you saying I have a sweet tooth?!

(ALL *laugh. Music begins.*)

MATT: Sam, you got the recipe? Lets hear it . . .

(*Lights up on choir. During song Media Club kids pantomime making brownies.*)

Recipe of Love

KATIE COMBS

NICK ROBERTSON
and KATIE COMBS
Arr. by Dave Clark

Lyrics:

It's a sweet, sweet thing, this rec-i-pe of love; It o-ver-flows with good-ness and its writ - ten from a - bove. It's a good, good thing and I'm

F
F
A

CD: 36

glad that I'm part of Con - sum - ing these great fla - vors in this

B♭
C

recipe of love. You take a quar - ter cup of __ pa -

F
F
Cm
A

- tience and you sprin - kle it with __ kind -

B♭
F
Cm
A

20
- ness. De - light your - self in the
B♭
C
22
truth but don't you think that you are through,
C
B♭7
24
my friend. You need a half a cup of good -
B♭7
F
Cm
A
26
- ness and a heap - ing scoop of hope -
B♭
F
Cm
A

54

Lyrics:

-ful - ness. Stir it up___ with___ trust,___

you'll___ find___ That this rec - i - pe stands___ the___ test___

of___ time.___ It's a sweet, sweet thing, this

rec - i - pe of love; It o - ver-flows with good - ness and is

Chord symbols: B♭, C, C, B♭7, B♭7, F, F/A, B♭, C

CD: 37 1st time
CD: 39 2nd time

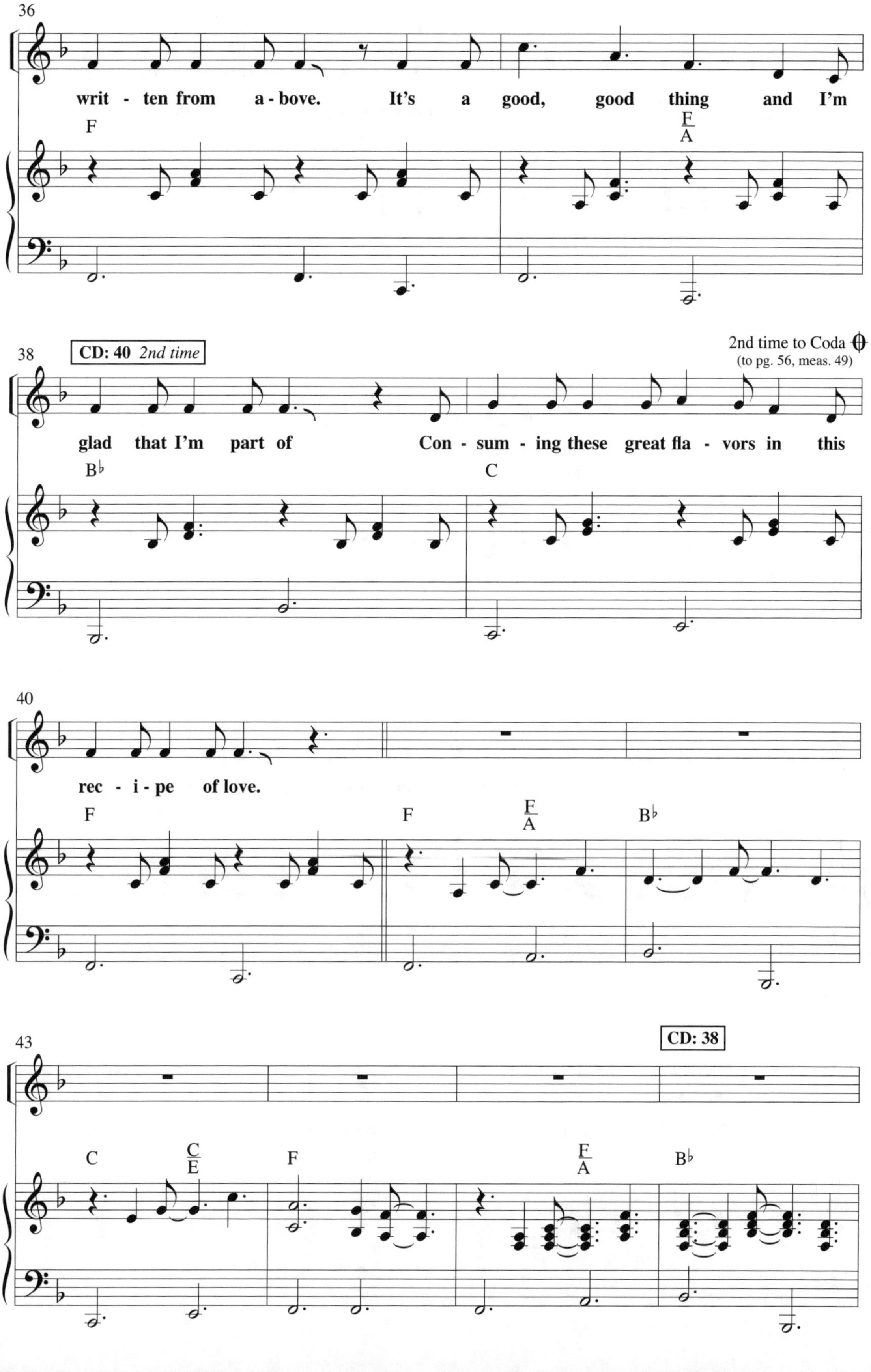
36
writ - ten from a - bove. It's a good, good thing and I'm
F
F/A
38
CD: 40 2nd time
2nd time to Coda
(to pg. 56, meas. 49)
glad that I'm part of Con - sum - ing these great fla - vors in this
B♭
C
40
rec - i - pe of love.
F
F
F/A
B♭
43
CD: 38
C
C/E
F
F/A
B♭

D.S. al Coda ⊕ CODA
(to pg. 52, meas. 17)

You take a rec - i - pe of love.

I can do all kinds of____ things____ but with - out love.____

CD: 41

I will not be sat - is - fied____ cause the

on - ly good things come from a - bove.____ It's a

58
sweet, sweet thing, this rec - i - pe of love; It
F F/A B♭
60
o - ver-flows with good - ness and its writ - ten from a-bove. It's a
C F
62
good, good thing and I'm glad that I'm part of Con -
F F/A B♭
64
sum - ing these great fla - vors in this rec - i - pe of love.
C F

(Fade to black. "Kids for Christ Theme Song" may be used to change out scene. Use the first few seconds and then fade out.)

Scene 5

(Lights up as kids enter Mega Media Clubhouse.)

CASEY: Well, I must say, that was the best project yet!

GRACE: It was certainly the yummiest!

JULIAN: Wow, it was crazy how excited those kids were to have us visit.

MATT: Yeah, we should go down there more often.

JULIAN *(holding video camera)*: Kerri, you ready to document this one?

KERRI: Sure!

JULIAN: You're on.

KERRI *(on camera)*: Well, this is our third entry. We made brownies for the kids at the Children's Center and boy, were they happy to see us. *(Music begins.)* I mean, we were just bringing them brownies, but you would have thought we were giving away Xboxes! So I guess today's "Leave a Mark" entry was the gift of . . . well, something little that meant something big!

(KIDS ad lib agreement as music begins. Lights up on choir. Choir wears sideways ball caps. See prop and movement ideas in the "Legacy of Love Director's Resource".)

A Little Means a Lot

Words and Music by
KATIE COMBS
Arr. by Dave Clark

9

lit-tle means a lot   if you start with some-thing,   Tak-ing what you got,   give it

F   C

all   from   love   and   You can do a small   thing and it   will   grow   till

C   G

12

it's   e - norm - ous.   And you nev-er know   what

C   Dm7   D#°7   C7/E   F

CD: 43 *1st time*

CD: 45 *2nd time*

it   will   lead   to,   Mak-ing oth-ers want   to   live   like   you   do,   A

F   C

15

lot from a lit - tle and it start-ed with a lit - tle from us. 1. A

G   C

17

big   oak tree___   start-ed from   a   seed___   so
2. You   don't have___   to   change   the world___   or

F   E m

19

sew   your seeds___   of   love.___
trav - el ver -   y   far.___

D m   C

21

You will find_____ that giv - en time_____ it's
Look a - round_____ and change the world_____ that's

F
Em

(to pg. 60, meas. 9)

CD: 44 *1st time*
CD: 46 *2nd time*

23

f

big - ger than you dreamed of._____
right in your own back - yard._____

A

Dm
$\frac{C}{E}$
F
$\frac{F}{G}$
G

f

26

lit - tle means a lot if you start with some - thing, Tak-ing what you got, give it

F
C

all from love and You can do a small thing and it will grow till

C   G

29

it's   e - norm - ous.   And you nev - er know what

C   Dm7   D#°7 $\frac{C^7}{E}$ F

CD: 47 *1st time*

it will lead to, Mak-ing oth - ers want to live like you do, A

F   C

32

lot from a lit - tle and it start-ed with a lit - tle from us.   An

G   C

mf

1

34

act of kind - ness, a word of en - cour - age - ment,

C   G   F   G

mf

36

help - ing those in need. A

C   G   F   G

38

CD: 48

friend - ly com - ment, an act of un - self - ish - ness

C   A m7   F   F/C   C

40

(to pg. 62, meas. 26)

f

2

plants a ti - ny seed. A us.

F   G   C   C

f

(Fade to black.)

Scene 6

(Lights up Mega Media Clubhouse. KIDS are hanging out. KERRI sits at the computer with the rest of the kids gathered around.)

KERRI: We still just need that one last thing . . . the thing that will push us over the top into the number one position.

GRACE: We are so close!

MATT: We've done all the things on our list.

CASEY: So, what's left?

JULIAN: We've done it all!

GRACE: That's pretty sad, you guys, that we can't think of more ways to leave a mark . . . it's only been a few days.

SAM *(starting to pace around the room)*: So, let's think . . . Christmas, gifts, giving, presents, lights . . . I've got it!

(SAM calls the kids over to a huddle they whisper for a moment.)

ALL: That's it!

(Lights out.)

Scene 7

(Lights up on Town Square. A nativity scene sits center. The kids arrive together.)

JULIAN: Hey, you got the lights?

CASEY *(carrying lights)*: Yeah, let's start over here. *(Music begins.)*

GRACE: Oh, look what I found! *(Walking over to the nativity scene)* Let's make this the center!

(Lights focus on nativity during first solo line. Lights up on choir as they join in at "O Little Town of Bethlehem". During the round portion of the song, the Mega Media Club kids string Christmas lights around the town square. Song ends with the solo as it began. All lights out except the newly placed Christmas lights and the Nativity spot. The Mega Media Club exits before song is over and takes position for Scene 8.)

(Optional: A two-sided mural comprised of large construction cards held by choir members to reveal a Bethlehem scene and star picture to be displayed during song. See the "Legacy of Love Director's Resource" for additional instructions.)

One Star

with
O Little Town of Bethlehem
Star of Wonder

KATIE COMBS

NICK ROBERTSON
and *KATIE COMBS*
Arr. by Dave Clark

CHOIR *unis.*

p

One star, one night, one world, one light;

G | Am/G | G | Am/G

CD: 51

One star I be-lieve a light can shine the

G | C² | G/D | D

mp   *"O Little Town of Bethlehem"

way. O lit - tle town of Beth - le -

G | Gsus | G | Am/G | G | Am/G | G | C/G

mp

hem, how still we see thee lie!

G | Gsus | G | Am/G | G | Am/G | G

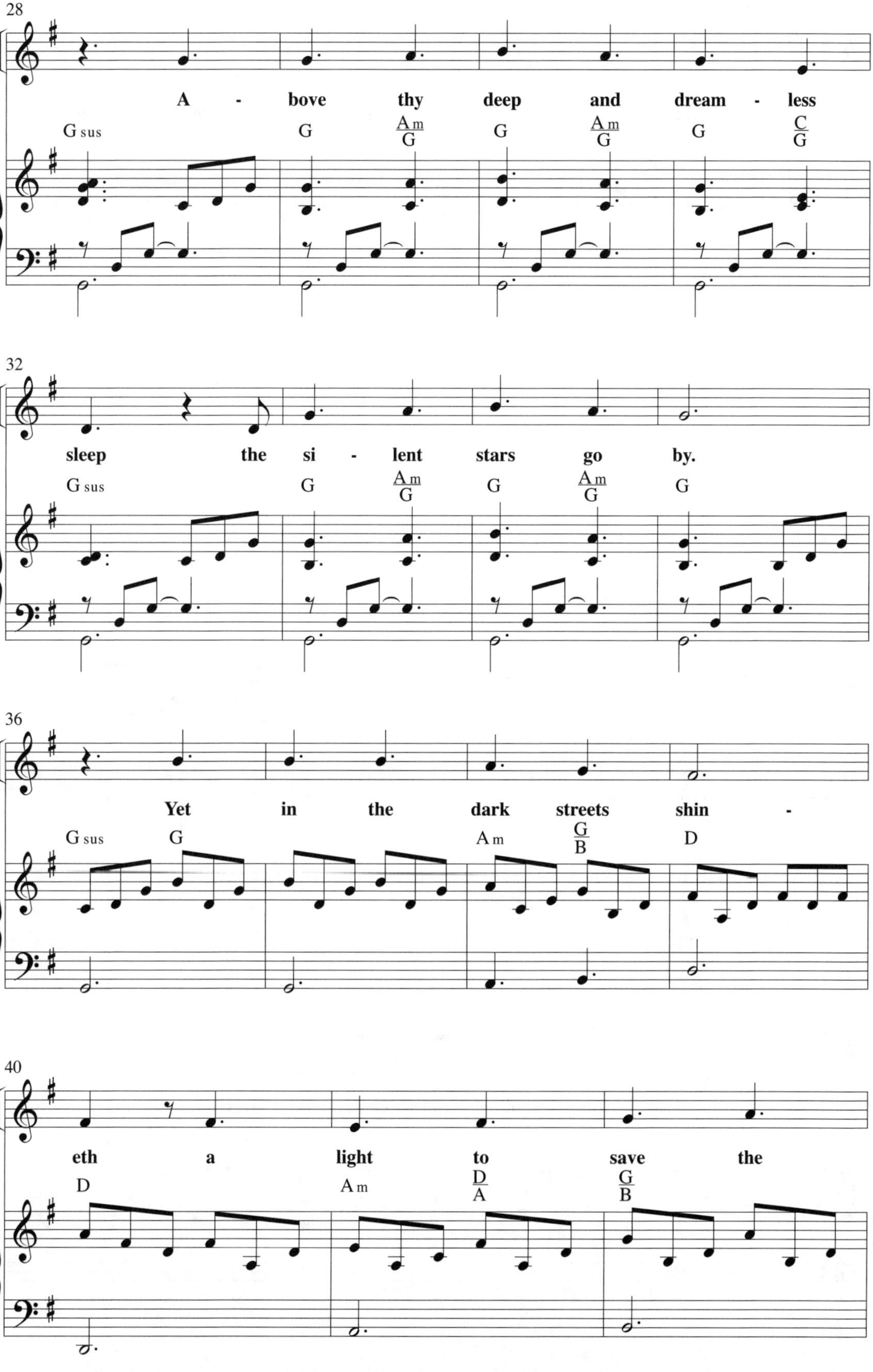
28
A - bove thy deep and dream - less
G sus G Am/G G Am/G G C/G
32
sleep the si - lent stars go by.
G sus G Am/G G Am/G G
36
Yet in the dark streets shin -
G sus G Am G/B D
40
eth a light to save the
D Am D/A G/B

CD: 52

world. One star, one night,

F² G Am/G

One world, one light; One star

G Am/G G

CD: 53

I be-lieve a light can shine the way. O

C² G/D D G G sus

SOLO
mp
One star, one night, one world, one light;

CHOIR *unis.*
lit - tle town of Beth - le - hem, how

One star I be - lieve a light___ can shine___ the
still we see thee lie!

way. One star, one night,
A - bove thy deep and

one world, one light; One star
dream - less sleep the si - lent

I be - lieve a light can shine the way.

stars go by.

*"Star of Wonder"
CHOIR unis.

Star of won - der, star of light, Star with roy - al

72
beau - ty bright, West - ward lead - ing, still pro - ceed - ing,
C G Em7 D C D
75
Guide us to thy per - fect light. Yet in the
G C G
78
dark streets shin - eth a
Am G/B D
CD: 55
81
light to save the world.
Am D/A G/B F2

One star, one night, one world, one light; One star I be-lieve a light___ can shine___ the way.

(Fade to black.)

Scene 8

(Lights up on Mega Media Clubhouse. KIDS, *except* MATT, *are hanging out.)*

KERRI: Wow, that was wonderful! What a night!

SAM: The town square looks magical!

CASEY: What time is it?

JULIAN: Almost time for the big announcement!

JOEY: Where's Mr. T?

GRACE: He's on his way. Matt is bringing him.

(MATT and MR. THOMPSON *enter)*

MR. THOMPSON: So what's this all about? What's this big surprise? And what have you kids been up to?

CASEY: Well, Mr. T, we have something to tell you. You see, we all wanted to get you a little something for Christmas . . .

KERRI: And the Kids for Christ webcast was holding a "Leave a Mark" contest.

GRACE: And the grand prize is a laptop computer! And we wanted to win it for you!

JULIAN: They are minutes away from announcing the winner!

MR. THOMPSON: Wow, kids. I don't know what to say! I'm flattered. I want you to know that whether or not you win . . .

JULIAN: I hate to interrupt you, Mr. T, but they are about to announce the big winner now!

(Music begins.)

Kids for Christ Theme Song (Short)

Music by
TIM HIGINBOTHAM
Arr. by Dave Clark

CD: 56

Funky ♩ = ca. 120

N.C.

(Lights up on Webcast Booth / Kids for Christ announcers.)

JIM: Good afternoon, kids, and welcome back to Kids for Christ. I'm Jim . . .

KRISTA: . . . And I'm Krista! And we know you've had a busy, busy week showing Christ's love to others! We've been flooded with literally hundreds of entries!

JIM: That's right, Krista . . . and remember, kids, no matter who wins this contest, you've done amazing work for God's kingdom. So give yourselves a big pat on the back for a job well done!

KRISTA: I'm not gonna pretend we're not all on pins and needles to find out the winner so I won't delay the big announcement . . . and the winner is . . .

JIM & KRISTA: The kids from Wikoma Washington Weekday Club!

JIM: Congratulations, kids!

KRISTA: But remember, you're all winners in Christ's eyes!

Kids for Christ Theme Song (Short)

Music by
TIM HIGINBOTHAM
Arr. by Dave Clark

Funky ♩ = ca. 120

CD: 56

(KIDS turn the webcast off and look dejected. Lights down on webcast booth.)

GRACE: I'm so sorry, Mr. Thompson.

JOEY: Yeah, we really tried hard.

MR. THOMPSON: Kids, come here and let me talk to you. What I was going to tell you before the big announcement is that I've already won. You doing all of this for me means more than winning any contest.

SAM: Huh?

MR. THOMPSON: You guys being a part of the Leave a Mark contest is like being a part of your own legacy of love.

MATT: Like what you told me the other day, about Mrs. Thompson and my grandma.

MR. THOMPSON: Right. But at Christmas time, we are reminded of the ultimate legacy of love in the gift of Jesus. He loves us perfectly, unconditionally, and He doesn't ask anything from us except for us to receive His love. *(Music begins)* And, what you guys did this week was to love others with that same kind of love. I'm so proud of you all.

(Lights up on choir.)

Legacy of Love
(Reprise)

KATIE COMBS

NICK ROBERTSON
and KATIE COMBS
Arr. by Dave Clark

Half-time feel ♩ = ca. 66

CD: 57

CHOIR *unis.*
mf

It's the

leg - a - cy___ of love___ and it's___ a - maz - ing;

12
And ev - er chang - ing as the sand a - long the shore.
G D/F♯ Em7 G2
15
And if you hold those mem - o - ries
Asus A Dsus
18
in - side your heart you take a hold of the gift,
D G A Bm
21
their leg - a - cy of love.
Em7 G2 A D

CD: 58

leg - a - cy___ that start - ed with___ a Sav - ior;___

mf There's a

The great - est gift___ the world___ has ev - er seen.___

A hope that bro't___ a light___ in-to___ the dark - ness;___ E - ter - nal life___ to all___ who would___ re - ceive. It's the leg - a - cy___ of love___

Chords: A sus | A | G2 | D/F# | E m7 | D/F# | C | G/B | A sus | Ab/Bb | Bb | Eb sus

CD: 59

cresc.

f

48 and it's ___ a - maz - ing;

50 And ev - er chang - ing as ___ the sand ___

52 a - long ___ the shore. ___

54 And if you hold those prom - is - es ___

in - side___ your heart you take___ a hold___

Eb Ab Bb

of___ the gift,___ their leg - a - cy___ of love.___

Cm Fm7 Ab2 Bb

Eb Ebsus

Eb Bb/C Cm Bb/Ab Ab/Bb Eb2

rit.

Christmas Groove
(Reprise*)

Words and Music by
KATIE COMBS
Arr. by Dave Clark

Got-ta jump, jump,— jump; got-ta move, move,— move. O you can't stand— still when the

*During reprise cast takes curtain calls and choir takes a bow. Take a moment here to recognize important helpers.

Spir - it__ moves__ you. Got-ta give love__ out, you got

noth-ing to__ lose; 'Cause Christ - mas puts__ you in the

CD: 62 *2nd time*

1st time: ALL
2nd time: GROUP 1

giv - in' groove.__ Slide in - to

2nd time: GROUP 2

Got-ta jump, jump,_ jump; Got-ta

14

gen - er - os - i - ty, swing_____ your heart

move, move,_ move; Swing, swing,_ swing; When the

F/A

Dm7

16

o - pen;_ Spin a - round___ and you___

Spir - it_ moves_ you. Got-ta give love_ out, you got

Gm7

Eb2

CD: 61 *1st time*

CD: 63 *2nd time*

18

_ will see___ that giv - ing leaves___ a leg -

noth-ing to_ lose. 'Cause Christ - mas puts_ you in the

Eb2

C/E

(to pg. 84, meas. 5)

20

-a - cy.___ Got-ta jump, jump,_ jump; got-ta

giv - in' groove.___ Got-ta jump, jump,_ jump; got-ta

C   F

22

move, move,_ move.   O you can't stand_ still   when the

Eb2   Gm7   F/A

24

Spir - it__ moves__ you. Got-ta give love__ out,   you got

Bb   Bb/C   F

noth-ing to__ lose; 'Cause Christ - mas puts__ you in the

giv - in' groove. So jump,

slide, spin, glide.

Come with me__ en - joy__ the ride.__

35

Sing a - long___ just one___ more time.___ Got-ta

37

jump, jump,___ jump; got-ta move, move,___ move. O you

39

can't stand___ still when the Spir - it___ moves___ you. Got-ta

CD: 66

41

give love___ out, you got noth-ing to___ lose; 'Cause

43

Christ - mas puts___ you in the giv - in' groove.___ Got-ta

G m7 | F/A | B♭/C | F

45

jump, jump,___ jump; got-ta move, move,___ move. O you

F | E♭2

47

can't stand___ still when the Spir - it___ moves___ you. Got-ta

G m7 | F/A | B♭ | B♭/C

49

give love___ out, you got noth-ing to___ lose; 'Cause

F | E♭2

CD: 67

Christ - mas puts___ you in the giv - in' groove.___ 'Cause

Christ - mas puts___ you in the giv - in' groove.___ 'Cause

Christ - mas puts___ you in the___

giv - in' groove.

Production Notes

For more details, tips and instructions on producing and directing Legacy of Love, please see the Director's Digital Resource CD-ROM and DVD combo (7-65762-00473-3) or the Demonstration DVD (7-65762-00453-3). Please call 1-800-363-2122 or visit www.lillenas.com to place your order.

Setting

The set for Legacy of Love is simple and does not require scene change. All that is needed is a classroom-type area for the Mega Media Clubhouse, and a small corner of the stage (blacked out through most of the production) serving as the Town Square for scene seven. The Webcast announcers can be hidden: on microphones voiceover-style or they can be placed on a separate part of the stage, framed out like they are inside a computer monitor.

Casting Ideas

This musical is developed to meet the needs of both large and small choirs. For smaller choirs, the entire choir can become part of the Mega Media Club. Larger choirs can feature smaller groups throughout songs. Special parts can be given to each interested child. Remember, to a child, passing out programs, getting a prop ready for a particular scene, or praying prior to the production is a big deal. It is important to make each child feel that they are a crucial part to this special ministry opportunity.

Special Movements

Movement instructions for each song can be found the Legacy of Love Director's Digital Resource or Demonstration DVD.

Costuming

The Mega Media Club members are all students at their local school. They can be dressed appropriate for the season. I recommend jeans and several layered shirts. They have four changes and will need to change in a split second so it is easiest for them to just peel a layer off.

The choir can wear seasonal clothing or order matching T-shirts for the show. You can order T-shirts specifically designed for Legacy of Love from:

        Personalized Gift and Apparel: Tom Roland, Owner (888) 898-6172
        Website: www.pg4u.com
        Email: info@pg4u.com

The Webcast hosts can be dressed snappy and seasonal.

Mr. Thompson should be dressed in a ridiculously outlandish Christmas outfit. Consider a blinking hat and obnoxious Christmas sweater. He will need three costume variations.

Set Design

For the Mega Media Clubhouse:
A door or entrance / exit area from the media center
Desk or table with several monitors
Classroom type décor-chalk, white or bulletin boards
Christmas decorations for the room
Some seating (couches, bean bags)
Oven or microwave oven (optional)
Risers for choir (optional)

For the Town Square:
Large nativity scene
Something to hang the lights from to light up the town square

Props

Sunglasses for choir (optional)
Ball caps for choir (optional)
Mural paper pieces for choir (optional)
Chef hats, mixing bowl, spoons, brownie mix boxes, kitchen stuff
Donation boxes or large baskets marked for: Toys, Clothes, Food, Kitchen stuff
Toys, clothes, food, kitchen items to go into the Donation Boxes

Microphone Needs

Cordless lavaliere microphones are ideal for the Mega Media Club members. Hand-held microphones can be used for the webcast hosts. A stationary microphone will be necessary for the song "One Star".

Scripture References

Christmas Groove

1 John 3:18 NIV

Dear children, let us not love with words or tongue but with actions and in truth.

Leave a Mark

Matthew 5:16 NIV

In the same way, let your light shine before men, that they may see your good deeds and praise your Father in heaven.

God's Done Bigger Things

Psalm 150:1-2 NIV

Praise the Lord. Praise God in his sanctuary; praise him in his mighty heavens. Praise him for his acts of power; praise him for his surpassing greatness.

Legacy of Love

John 3:16 NIV

For God so loved the world that he gave his one and only Son, that whoever believes in him shall not perish but have eternal life.

Little Bit of Stuff

Matt 6:19-21 NIV

Do not store up for yourselves treasures on earth, where moth and rust destroy, and where thieves break in and steal. But store up for yourselves treasures in heaven, where moth and rust do not destroy, and where thieves do not break in and steal. For where your treasure is, there your heart will be also.

Recipe of Love

1 Corinthians 13:4-7 NIV

Love is patient, love is kind. It does not envy, it does not boast, it is not proud. It is not rude, it is not self-seeking, it is not easily angered, it keeps no record of wrongs. Love does not delight in evil but rejoices with the truth. It always protects, always trusts, always hopes, always perseveres.

A Little Means a Lot

Colossians 3:23-24 NIV

Whatever you do, work at it with all your heart, as working for the Lord, not for men, since you know that you will receive an inheritance from the Lord as a reward. It is the Lord Christ you are serving.

One Star

John 1:9 NIV

The true light that gives light to every man was coming into the world.

Legacy of Love

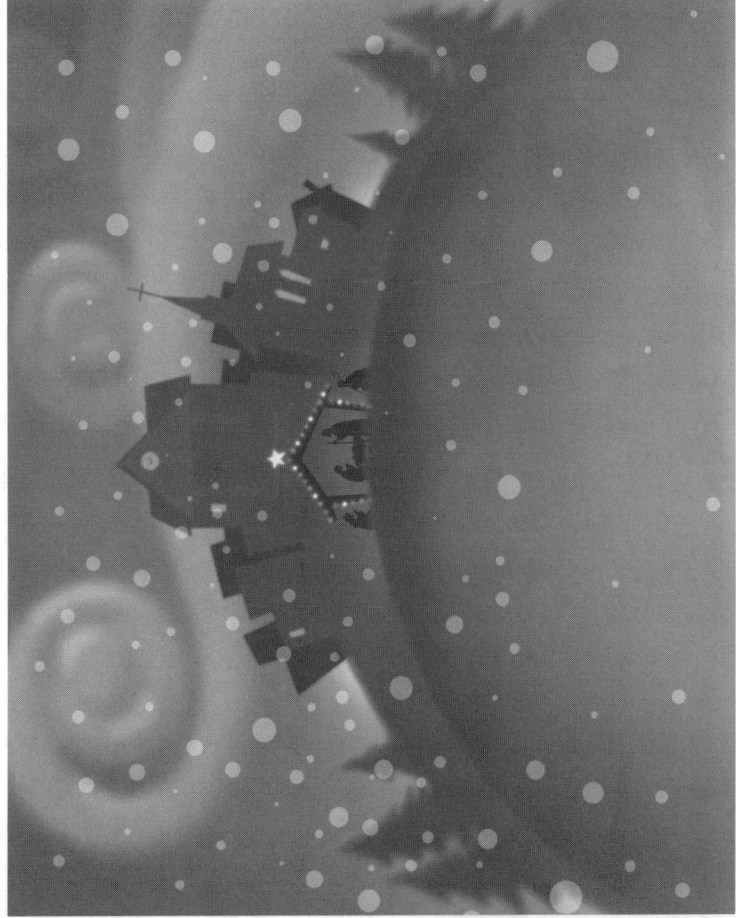

Legacy of Love

Legacy of Love